STATES

DELAWARE

A MyReportLinks.com Book

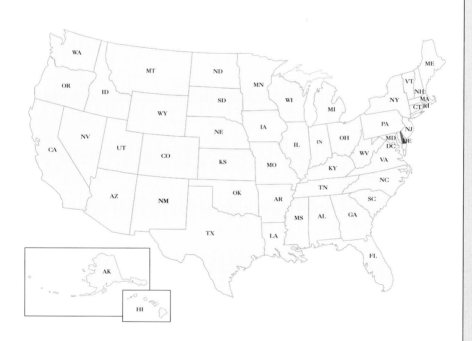

Chris Reiter

MyReportLinks.com Books

an imprint of

Enslow Publishers, Inc.

Box 398, 40 Industrial Road
Berkeley Heights, NJ 07922
USA

MyReportLinks.com Books, an imprint of Enslow Publishers, Inc. MyReportLinks is a trademark of Enslow Publishers, Inc.

Library of Congress Cataloging-in-Publication Data

Reiter, Chris.
    Delaware / Chris Reiter.
        p. cm. — (States)
    Summary: Discusses the land and climate, economy, government, and
    history of the second smallest state in the nation. Includes Internet
    links to Web sites, source documents, and photographs related to
    Delaware.
    Includes bibliographical references and index.
    ISBN 0-7660-5019-X
    1. Delaware—Juvenile literature. [1. Delaware.] I. Title. II. States
(Series : Berkeley Heights, N.J.)
F164.3 .R45 2002
975.1—dc21
                                    2002000117

Printed in the United States of America

10 9 8 7 6 5 4 3 2 1

To Our Readers:
Through the purchase of this book, you and your library gain access to the Report Links that specifically back up this book.

The Publisher will provide access to the Report Links that back up this book and will keep these Report Links up to date on **www.myreportlinks.com** for three years from the book's first publication date.

We have done our best to make sure all Internet addresses in this book were active and appropriate when we went to press. However, the author and the Publisher have no control over, and assume no liability for, the material available on those Internet sites or on other Web sites they may link to.

The usage of the MyReportLinks.com Books Web site is subject to the terms and conditions stated on the Usage Policy Statement on **www.myreportlinks.com**.

In the future, a password may be required to access the Report Links that back up this book. The password is found on the bottom of page 4 of this book.

Any comments or suggestions can be sent by e-mail to comments@myreportlinks.com or to the address on the back cover.

Photo Credits: ©Corel Corporation, pp. 3 (Constitution, Library of Congress), 10; Courtesy Delaware Tourism Office, pp. 13, 14, 16, 26, 30, 36, 38; Courtesy MyReportLinks.com Books, p. 4; Courtesy of Delaware State Museums, pp. 34, 41; Courtesy of Delaware State Parks, p. 29; Courtesy of Delaware Wildflowers, p. 18; Courtesy of The Delaware Audubon Society, p. 22; Courtesy of The Delaware Estuary Program, p. 20; Courtesy of The DuPont Company, p. 25; Courtesy of The State of Delaware, p. 32; Courtesy of The Swedish Colonial Society, p. 39; Courtesy of The U.S. Army Corps of Engineers, p. 23.

Cover Photo: Courtesy Delaware Office of Tourism

Cover Description: The re-created tall ship *Kalmar Nyckel*, Wilmington

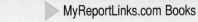
Contents

MyReportLinks.com Books
Great Books, Great Links, Great for Research!

MyReportLinks.com Books present the information you need to learn about your report subject. In addition, they show you where to go on the Internet for more information. The pre-evaluated Report Links that back up this book are kept up to date on **www.myreportlinks.com**. With the purchase of a MyReportLinks.com Books title, you and your library gain access to the Report Links that specifically back up that book. The Report Links save hours of research time and link to dozens—even hundreds—of Web sites, source documents, and photos related to your report topic.

Please see "To Our Readers" on the Copyright page for important information about this book, the MyReportLinks.com Books Web site, and the Report Links that back up this book.

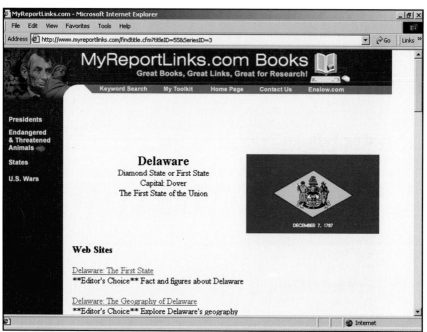

Access:

The Publisher will provide access to the Report Links that back up this book and will try to keep these Report Links up to date on our Web site for three years from the book's first publication date. Please enter **SDE1955** if asked for a password.

Report Links

 The Internet sites described below can be accessed at
http://www.myreportlinks.com

*EDITOR'S CHOICE

▶ Delaware: The First State

This Web site features fun facts and trivia about Delaware. You will also find biographies, current events, and images relating to Delaware.

Link to this Internet site from http://www.myreportlinks.com

*EDITOR'S CHOICE

▶ Delaware: The Geography of Delaware

This Web site contains detailed information about Delaware's geography, including its major rivers, highest points, and bordering states. You can also view a close-up map of Delaware.

Link to this Internet site from http://www.myreportlinks.com

*EDITOR'S CHOICE

▶ Delaware Biographies

At this Web site you will find the biographies of some of Delaware's leaders including biographies of Caesar Rodney, George Read, and John McKinly.

Link to this Internet site from http://www.myreportlinks.com

*EDITOR'S CHOICE

▶ The Founding Fathers: Delegates to the Constitutional Convention

At the National Archives and Records Administration Web site you can read the biographies of Delaware's five delegates to the Constitutional Convention.

Link to this Internet site from http://www.myreportlinks.com

*EDITOR'S CHOICE

▶ Delaware.gov

At this Web site you can explore local government in Delaware and learn about Delaware's governor.

Link to this Internet site from http://www.myreportlinks.com

*EDITOR'S CHOICE

▶ Explore the States: Delaware

America's Story from America's Library, a Library of Congress Web site, provides interesting facts about Delaware. You will also find links to other sites about Delaware.

Link to this Internet site from http://www.myreportlinks.com

Report Links

The Internet sites described below can be accessed at
http://www.myreportlinks.com

▶ **Annie Jump Cannon**
At this Web site you will find a biography of Annie Jump Cannon, daughter of a Delaware shipbuilder and state senator, who became a noted physicist and astronomer.

Link to this Internet site from http://www.myreportlinks.com

▶ **A Brief History of New Sweden in America**
This Web site offers a brief history of New Sweden, including its beginnings at Fort Christina, the first permanent settlement in the Delaware Valley.

Link to this Internet site from http://www.myreportlinks.com

▶ **The Chesapeake and Delaware Canal**
At this Web site you can explore the history of the Chesapeake and Delaware Canal, the nation's busiest sea-level canal.

Link to this Internet site from http://www.myreportlinks.com

▶ **Crossing the Delaware!**
This Web site offers facts about the history, design, and construction of the Chesapeake and Delaware Canal Bridge.

Link to this Internet site from http://www.myreportlinks.com

▶ **Delaware Division of Parks and Recreation**
At this Web site you can explore the parks of Delaware and learn about archaeological digs in the state. You can also navigate through an interactive map of Delaware, which gives a brief overview of Delaware's parks.

Link to this Internet site from http://www.myreportlinks.com

▶ **The Delaware Estuary Program**
This Web site provides information about the Delaware Estuary, an environmentally important body of water that supports fish, shellfish, and marine mammals as well as other living things. Learn about the efforts to keep the 133-mile-long estuary free of pollution.

Link to this Internet site from http://www.myreportlinks.com

The Internet sites described below can be accessed at
http://www.myreportlinks.com

▶ **Delaware History—The Delaware Indians**
These pages offer a detailed history of the Delaware, or Lenape, Indians,
an Algonquian tribe whose members lived on lands that today form the
Mid-Atlantic region of the United States.

Link to this Internet site from http://www.myreportlinks.com

▶ **Delaware Maps**
The Perry-Castañeda Library at the University of Texas at Austin holds
a collection of maps of Delaware. Here you will find maps of the state,
its cities, and historical maps.

Link to this Internet site from http://www.myreportlinks.com

▶ **Delaware State Museums**
Take a virtual tour of Delaware's state museums, where you can explore
Delaware's part in the Underground Railroad and Civil War and learn
about the state's horticulture, among other things.

Link to this Internet site from http://www.myreportlinks.com

▶ **Delaware Wildflowers**
At the Delaware Wildflower Web site you can learn about and see
images of wildflowers that are native to Delaware.

Link to this Internet site from http://www.myreportlinks.com

▶ **The Delaware Symphony Orchestra**
The Delaware Symphony Orchestra Web site offers information
about the orchestra's history, including its beginnings as the
Tankopanicum Orchestra, founded by Alfred I. duPont.

Link to this Internet site from http://www.myreportlinks.com

▶ **DuPont Overview**
At the DuPont Company Web site you can learn about the company's
long history and view a time line of the company's evolution from 1802
to the present.

Link to this Internet site from http://www.myreportlinks.com

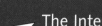

Report Links

▶ Fort Delaware Society

At this Web site you will find information about Fort Delaware, including a brief history of the fort and historical images.

Link to this Internet site from http://www.myreportlinks.com

▶ George Read

At this Web site you will find a brief biography of George Read, one of Delaware's signers of the Declaration of Independence.

Link to this Internet site from http://www.myreportlinks.com

▶ Historical Society of Delaware

By navigating through the Historical Society of Delaware's Web site you will discover interesting facts about Delaware. Also featured at this Web site is a section about Delaware women and the suffrage movement.

Link to this Internet site from http://www.myreportlinks.com

▶ Horseshoe Crabs Given Sanctuary

At this Web site you will learn about the current legislation banning the capture of horseshoe crabs. You will also find links to more information about horseshoe crabs and their habitat.

Link to this Internet site from http://www.myreportlinks.com

▶ The Nanticoke People

These pages explore the history of the Nanticoke Indians, a confederacy of tribes that once controlled much of the Delmarva Peninsula. The Nanticoke Indian tribe of Delaware is today based in Sussex County, Delaware, with tribal members across the country.

Link to this Internet site from http://www.myreportlinks.com

▶ Oliver Evans—Inventor

Born in Delaware in 1755, Oliver Evans invented a steam-powered wagon. This site provides a brief history of the steam engine and biographical information about Oliver Evans.

Link to this Internet site from http://www.myreportlinks.com

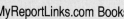
Report Links

→ The Internet sites described below can be accessed at
http://www.myreportlinks.com

▶ **The River Basin**
At this Web site you can explore the three regions of the Delaware
watershed: the Uplands, Piedmont, and the Estuary. You will also find
detailed information about these areas by clicking on the map provided.

Link to this Internet site from http://www.myreportlinks.com

▶ **State of Delaware (A Brief History)**
At this Web site you will find a brief history of Delaware, including
facts about early explorations of Delaware's coastline and Delaware's
efforts to ratify the Constitution.

Link to this Internet site from http://www.myreportlinks.com

▶ **Stately Knowledge: Delaware**
At this Web site you will find facts about Delaware, links to
encyclopedias and almanacs with information about Delaware,
and other useful Web sites about Delaware.

Link to this Internet site from http://www.myreportlinks.com

▶ **Thomas McKean**
This Web site provides a brief biography of Thomas McKean, one of
Delaware's signers of the Declaration of Independence. Here you will
learn about his education and political involvement in Delaware.

Link to this Internet site from http://www.myreportlinks.com

▶ **U.S. Census Bureau: Delaware**
At the U.S. Census Bureau Web site you will find quick facts relating
to the 2000 Census, including information about Delaware's people,
businesses, and geography.

Link to this Internet site from http://www.myreportlinks.com

▶ **Welcome to Delaware**
The official Web site of the Delaware Tourism Office offers an
exploration of the history, culture, and attractions of the state.
An online quiz is also offered.

Link to this Internet site from http://www.myreportlinks.com

Delaware Facts

▶ **Capital**
Dover

▶ **Population**
783,600*

▶ **Bird**
Blue hen chicken

▶ **Tree**
American holly

▶ **Flower**
Peach blossom

▶ **Fish**
Weakfish

▶ **Insect**
Ladybug

▶ **Mineral**
Sillimanite

▶ **Song**
"Our Delaware"

▶ **Motto**
Liberty and independence

▶ **Nicknames**
The Blue Hen State; The Diamond State; The First State; Small Wonder

DECEMBER 7, 1787

▶ **Flag**
The flag's background of colonial blue surrounds a diamond of buff color. In the diamond is the coat of arms of the state, and below it the date "December 7, 1787," which refers to the day on which Delaware ratified the U.S. Constitution, becoming the first state to do so. The shades of blue and buff represent shades that were present in a uniform worn by General George Washington during the American Revolution.

*Population reflects the 2000 census.

The State of Delaware

Delaware is perhaps best known for being one of the nation's smallest states. Its population is 783,600 (2000 U.S. census), a smaller population than that of most big cities. The state's three counties cover just 1,955 square miles,[1] an area smaller than that of many national parks. In fact, Delaware would fit into the state of Texas twenty-seven times! Only tiny Rhode Island is smaller.

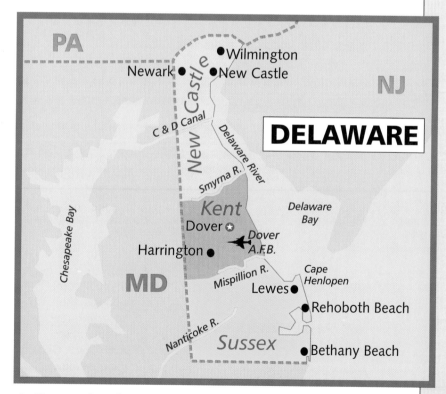

▲ The second smallest state in the United States, Delaware is only 100 miles long and 35 miles wide at its widest point.

But little Delaware is also proof that bigger is *not* necessarily better. Within its borders are pristine beaches, seaside resorts, and great fishing. There are acres of fertile farmland, too, as well as thriving high-tech industries and sites of historic importance. So proud are Delawareans of their state that they call it a "small wonder." And it is.

Delaware is in the Middle Atlantic region of the eastern United States. Pennsylvania is its northern neighbor, Maryland borders Delaware to the west and south, and New Jersey is Delaware's eastern neighbor across Delaware Bay. Also to the east are the waters of the Atlantic Ocean, the Delaware Bay, and the Delaware River. The tides, currents, and shores of these bodies of water have shaped Delaware's history and continue to give the state much of its character and natural beauty.

▶ Delaware's Beaches

During the summer, tourists flock to Delaware's beaches. On summer evenings, many visit the boardwalk at Rehoboth Beach, where there are rides, arcades, and games. The Delaware shore draws so many visitors from Washington, D.C., that Rehoboth Beach has come to be called "the nation's summer capital."

The Delaware coast is popular with the animal kingdom, too. Just north of Rehoboth is Cape Henlopen, where the Atlantic Ocean meets the Delaware Bay. Birds and other wildlife thrive on the cape's quiet beaches, dunes, and marshes. Great blue herons wade in the wetlands. Foxes den in the dunes and pine forests. Ospreys, sometimes known as fish hawks, dive for fish swimming on the surface of the bay.

▲ *The seaside resort of Rehoboth Beach features a mile-long boardwalk; wide, sandy beaches; museums; amusements; and water sports of all kinds.*

▶ Food for the Trip North

Cape Henlopen is also the site of an amazing spring ritual. In mid-May, horseshoe crabs crawl out of the sea to lay millions of eggs on the beach. As the horseshoe crabs lay their eggs, migrating shorebirds, on their way from South America to their breeding grounds in the Arctic, land on the cape. For many of the birds, Cape Henlopen is their only stop. Every year they arrive just in time to devour the horseshoe crab eggs. The eggs provide the birds with enough stored energy to make the second half of their long flight north. Somehow they know just when to arrive at Cape Henlopen. If they are wrong by even a few days, they might not survive the flight home.[2] But they are rarely

wrong. It seems that both birds and humans know where to find their snacks on the Delaware shore.

▶ A Rich History

Not far from Cape Henlopen is the seaside town of Lewes, the site of Delaware's first European settlement. In 1631, only eleven years after the English arrived at Plymouth Rock, Dutch settlers landed in Lewes. They called their new settlement *Zwaanendael*, Dutch for "valley of the swans." One of the early settlers described the flat landscape surrounding Lewes as "beautifully level."[3]

In historic Lewes, signs of early settlement have survived. Old houses, churches, and gravestones tell the story of another time. A cannonball from a Revolutionary War bombardment still rests in the brick foundation of a building facing the bay. Sometimes a restored eighteenth-century sailing vessel is tied up at the town dock. In Lewes, it's easy to imagine the many places where European settlers got their start.

Some of Delaware's settlers became American patriots. During the Revolutionary War, Delawareans Caesar Rodney, Thomas McKean, and George Read were delegates to the Continental Congress. All of the Delaware delegates signed the Declaration of Independence.

◀ *The Zwaanendael Museum, in Lewes, was designed to resemble a city hall in the Netherlands. The museum offers visitors a glimpse into southeastern Delaware life from the sixteenth century to the present.*

After the American Revolution, the delegates from each state worked on the United States Constitution, which established the American system of government. After the document was written, the delegates returned a copy of the Constitution to their home states to allow their local governments to review it. On December 7, 1787, the Delaware Assembly was the first to approve the U.S. Constitution. Delaware had thus become the first state in the new United States.

Delaware's First Family

Rodney, McKean, and Read were the first patriots of the first state, but the du Ponts are, in many ways, considered Delaware's first family. They weren't the first family to live in Delaware, but they have been first in business, industry, and government for many years.

The du Pont dynasty started with a gunpowder mill near Wilmington. It supplied the young nation with powder. Thomas Jefferson was one of the mill's customers, buying powder to clear the land near his Virginia home.[4] From the powder mill, the du Pont family developed one of the world's most successful chemical companies. By the twentieth century, E.I. du Pont de Nemours and Company, known more simply as DuPont, had become an industrial giant with a reputation for creating innovative products and materials.

As DuPont grew, northern Delaware grew. Many people found good jobs with the company, and many more moved to Delaware in search of employment. Other industries grew on DuPont's coattails. By the 1930s, Delaware—little Delaware—had become one of the nation's most prosperous states.

Chapter 2 ▶

Land and Climate

Delaware lies just about halfway between Florida and Maine on the Atlantic coast. People who live in southern states often think of Delaware as a northern state, and most people from the north think of Delaware as part of the south. In a way, both are right. Delaware's bald cypress trees are typically found much farther south. And many rural Delawareans in Sussex County speak with a slight southern accent. But the rolling hills of northern Delaware look very much like those found in New England.

Delaware is also a blend of rural and urban landscapes. Wilmington, Delaware, in the northern part of the state, is

▲ Part of Trap Pond State Park, in the southwestern part of the state, Trussom Pond features bald cypress trees, which are usually found much farther south.

the largest city in Delaware, with a population of 72,664 (2000 census). Wilmington is a short train ride away from Philadelphia, one of America's largest cities. But Wilmington is equally close to farmland and marshland preserves south of the city, and just a two-hour drive from almost anywhere in the state.

For most people, the Delaware River and Delaware Bay are the defining natural features of the state. And because Delaware is only 35 miles wide at its widest point, whether you are in city, town, or countryside, you are never far from the water.

Delaware today is a state in which most people live in suburbs. With a population of 783,600, fewer than 200,000 people live in cities or towns, and fewer than 100,000 people live in rural areas. In many ways, this distribution of population resembles that of the rest of America.

▶ Climate

Because Delaware borders the Atlantic Ocean, the state's climate is moderate. Average monthly temperatures in Wilmington in January are 31°F and in July, 76°F.[1] On most days, temperatures near the ocean are about 10 degrees cooler in summer and 10 degrees warmer in winter than areas just a few miles inland. The average annual precipitation is about 45 inches. The growing season in Delaware is six to seven months in most years.

Despite the moderate climate, severe storms can and do occur in Delaware. The state has seen its share of blizzards when a storm tracks up the East Coast from the south. For residents living near the ocean, northeasters and hurricanes are a more serious threat. Many times in the past one hundred years, major hurricanes have passed

over or near Delaware. Some of the more memorable were Hazel in 1954, Diane in 1955, Donna in1960, and Grace in 1991.

▶ Geographic Regions

Nearly the entire state is located on the Atlantic Coastal Plain, except the northern tip, which is in the Piedmont Plateau. The coastal plain extends most of the length of the East Coast of the United States. It is the flat, fertile land between the ocean and the foothills, or piedmont, of the Appalachian Mountains. So much of Delaware lies in this lowland plain that its mean elevation is only 60 feet

There are more than 1,500 plant species native to Delaware. These wildflowers were photographed at various places in New Castle County, including the Middle Run Valley Natural Area.

above sea level, making Delaware the lowest state in the entire country.

The northern region of Delaware includes the state's highest point, an elevation of 447.85 feet above sea level near Ebright Road, in New Castle County.[2] Heading south, the rolling hills give way to pastureland toward the center of the state. In the south the land is a mixture of marsh, farmland, and upland forest. The coast features extensive marshland along the Delaware Bay, which meets the Atlantic Ocean at Cape Henlopen. Cape Henlopen was once named Cape De La Warr in honor of Thomas West, Lord De La Warr, the first colonial governor of Virginia. The Delaware River, which flows into the bay from the north, took its name from the cape. South of Cape Henlopen are Delaware's popular beaches, backed by sand dunes and inland bays.

Land

Like most coastal states, Delaware was almost completely forested when European explorers arrived. However, the demands of settlers for building materials and agricultural land reduced the forest to about one third of the state. The northern part of the state features mixed hardwoods. Oak and hickory are the most common. In central Delaware, coastal hardwoods give way to loblolly pine. Sussex County, in southern Delaware, features extensive stands of pine surrounded by even larger forests of mixed hardwoods (black walnut, sweetgum, tulip poplar) and pine.[3] Shadbush and sassafras trees are common in the south as well.

Agricultural land is more common today in Sussex and Kent Counties than in New Castle County. Driving the back roads of Sussex County at night, the lights from

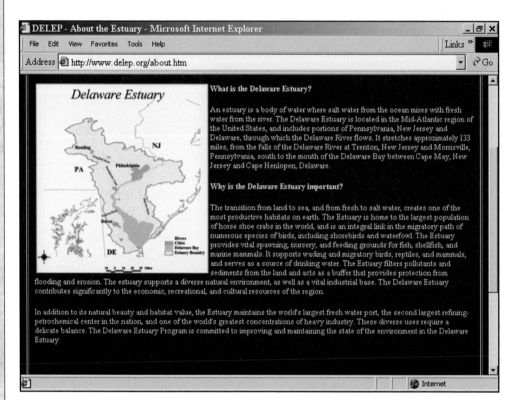

DELEP - About the Estuary - Microsoft Internet Explorer

File   Edit   View   Favorites   Tools   Help   Links »

Address http://www.delep.org/about.htm   Go

Delaware Estuary

What is the Delaware Estuary?

An estuary is a body of water where salt water from the ocean mixes with fresh water from the river. The Delaware Estuary is located in the Mid-Atlantic region of the United States, and includes portions of Pennsylvania, New Jersey and Delaware, through which the Delaware River flows. It stretches approximately 133 miles, from the falls of the Delaware River at Trenton, New Jersey and Morrisville, Pennsylvania, south to the mouth of the Delaware Bay between Cape May, New Jersey and Cape Henlopen, Delaware.

Why is the Delaware Estuary important?

The transition from land to sea, and from fresh to salt water, creates one of the most productive habitats on earth. The Estuary is home to the largest population of horse shoe crabs in the world, and is an integral link in the migratory path of numerous species of birds, including shorebirds and waterfowl. The Estuary provides vital spawning, nursery, and feeding grounds for fish, shellfish, and marine mammals. It supports wading and migratory birds, reptiles, and mammals, and serves as a source of drinking water. The Estuary filters pollutants and sediments from the land and acts as a buffer that provides protection from flooding and erosion. The estuary supports a diverse natural environment, as well as a vital industrial base. The Delaware Estuary contributes significantly to the economic, recreational, and cultural resources of the region.

In addition to its natural beauty and habitat value, the Estuary maintains the world's largest fresh water port, the second largest refining-petrochemical center in the nation, and one of the world's greatest concentrations of heavy industry. These diverse uses require a delicate balance. The Delaware Estuary Program is committed to improving and maintaining the state of the environment in the Delaware Estuary.

Internet

The Delaware Estuary, a body of water which extends from New Jersey to Cape Henlopen, Delaware, provides a habitat for many species of wading and migratory birds, mammals, and reptiles, and is also home to the world's largest freshwater port.

farmhouses still twinkle much the way they did two hundred years ago. On a fall day, standing at the edge of a cornfield or near a salt marsh in Sussex County, one is more likely to see deer prancing by or ducks flying south than people.

The coastal areas feature various grasses that thrive along the sand dunes. These grasses are important because they help to anchor the dunes and keep them from being completely washed away by tidal flooding. Still, beach erosion is an ongoing problem along the coast. In some areas, programs are under way to replenish beaches by pumping sand from off shore. More attention is being given to the preservation of marshes and wetlands as well, which are the habitat for many species of birds and mammals. It will also preserve resting and feeding areas for migrating birds such as Canada geese and shorebirds such as red knots, ruddy turnstones, and sandpipers. Many of these birds visit Delaware's two large national wildlife refuges, Prime Hook and Bombay Hook. Both are excellent places to view bird migrations.[4]

▶ Animals

The white-tailed deer is the only large mammal found in Delaware. Smaller mammals such as foxes, red and gray squirrels, rabbits, and muskrats are common. Many species of shorebirds make Delaware home, too. Their main source of food, the horseshoe crab, is in fact not a crab at all, but rather a relative of the scorpion and the spider. The horseshoe crab may be the single most important animal species found in Delaware.

Along with laying billions of eggs that provide food for migrating birds, Delaware's horseshoe crabs support a variety of human enterprises. The crabs' shells can be ground up to make fertilizer for farms and mixed with other ingredients to make food for hogs and chickens. Their legs make excellent bait for people fishing for eels and conches.

Science, too, is served by the horseshoe crab. For the last fifty years, much of what we know about the human eye has come as a result of studying the compound eye of the horseshoe crab. And chitin, a substance found in the shells of horseshoe crabs, is used to heal burns. The crabs' blood contains a clotting agent called lysate, which attaches to bacteria. Lysate is so effective at identifying

DAS ONLINE: Horseshoe Crab Sanctuary - Microsoft Internet Explorer

File Edit View Favorites Tools Help   Links »

Address http://www.delawareaudubon.org/conservation/sanctuary.html   Go

Horseshoe Crabs Given Sanctuary by National Marine Fisheries Service

The National Marine Fisheries Service of the National Oceanic and Atmospheric Administration (NOAA) has banned fishing for horseshoe crabs in federal waters off the mouth of the Delaware Bay. The agency published a final rule that will implement the closed area effective March 7, 2001.

This ban provides additional protection for local stocks and helps to ensure that declining populations of migratory shorebirds will have an abundant source of horseshoe crab eggs to feed on when they stop to rest in the Delaware Bay before flying north to their Canadian nesting areas.

All of the affected Atlantic Coast states, including Delaware, have reduced their horseshoe crab bait catch by 25% under guidelines established by the Atlantic States Marine Fisheries Commission in its horseshoe crab fishery management plan. The ASMFC also recommended a prohibition on fishing for horseshoe crabs in federal waters within a 30-nautical-mile radius of the mouth of the Delaware Bay.

Under the new rule, the area closed to fishing for horseshoe crabs is roughly rectangular in shape and encompasses about 1,500 square miles of federal waters. It adjoins state waters south of Pecks Beach, NJ, to just north of Ocean City, MD. It is designated as the "Carl N. Schuster Jr. Horseshoe Crab Reserve," in honor of the retired William and Mary College professor, who is considered a leading horseshoe crab biologist and researcher.

"The closure will offer protection for horseshoe crabs in federal waters, particularly for the Delaware Bay stock," said Bill Hogarth, acting director of NOAA Fisheries. "Improving protection for horseshoe crabs will promote long-term sustainability for fisheries that depend on horseshoe crabs for bait, research and medical purposes, and ensure an ample supply of horseshoe crab eggs for food for migratory shorebirds."

John Bianchi, Senior Policy Advisor at the National Audubon Society, commented that "This final action comes in the

Done   Internet

The largest population of horseshoe crabs in the world is found in the Delaware Bay and Estuary. The crabs' eggs provide food for the millions of migratory shorebirds that stop to feed in Delaware Bay on their long journey north to Canada to their nesting grounds.

bacteria that all new drugs are now tested for purity with horseshoe crab blood. Research involving horseshoe crabs has led to three scientists winning the Nobel Prize. With so much attention paid them, the crabs are now being carefully watched to make sure that they remain plentiful.[5]

The real lesson to be learned from the humble horseshoe crab is that all things, even the smallest, are important. The land of Delaware provides many opportunities to observe that phenomenon.

Chapter 3

Economy

From colonial times to the present, the economy of Delaware has centered primarily around the city of Wilmington. Its location on the Brandywine River near that river's confluence with the deepwater Delaware River attracted manufacturing, and the manufacturing economy fueled a growing commerce between Delaware and New

▲ The Chesapeake and Delaware Canal is the nation's busiest canal at sea level. Constructed in the 1820s, it soon brought more shipping to Delaware and was responsible for the growth of Delaware's largest city, Wilmington, in the nineteenth century.

York. Early commerce centered on leather goods, shipbuilding, farm products, and milled flour.[1] The latter received a major boost in 1785 when Delawarean Oliver Evans invented an automatic flour milling machine.[2]

The Chesapeake and Delaware Canal

The first major project to have an economic impact on Delaware was the Chesapeake and Delaware Canal. Built between 1824 and 1829, it connected the Chesapeake Bay in Maryland with the Delaware Bay in Delaware. It greatly reduced the distance of the water route between Baltimore and Philadelphia. Canal shipping helped Wilmington to grow by increasing the level of shipping traffic on the Delaware River. The C&D Canal, as it is commonly known, is the "oldest major commercial waterway still in use" in the United States.[3]

In 1838 a railroad opened between Philadelphia and Baltimore that brought train traffic through Wilmington. This made it even easier to transport goods and people between the three cities. Among the agricultural products to be shipped were corn, wheat, and, especially, peaches. In fact, at one time Delaware was known as the "Peach State."

The DuPont Impact

One of the most important events in Delaware's economic history occurred in 1802. That year, E.I. du Pont de Nemours, who had arrived in Delaware from France, established a gunpowder factory near Wilmington. From the beginning, the business grew rapidly. By 1811, DuPont was the largest manufacturer of gunpowder in America. Early in the twentieth century, DuPont began to expand into a major chemical company.[4] In 1912 the explosives business was so large that the United States Supreme Court ordered DuPont split into three separate companies in order to promote competition. Despite this move by the Court, the company remained large enough to buy the automaker General Motors in the 1920s and control it for a number of years.

Eventually, the company moved beyond manufacturing chemicals and began using them to create or enhance other products. The results were spectacular. Synthetic rubber for better tires, nylon for clothing, and freon for appliances all helped create vast new related industries.[5]

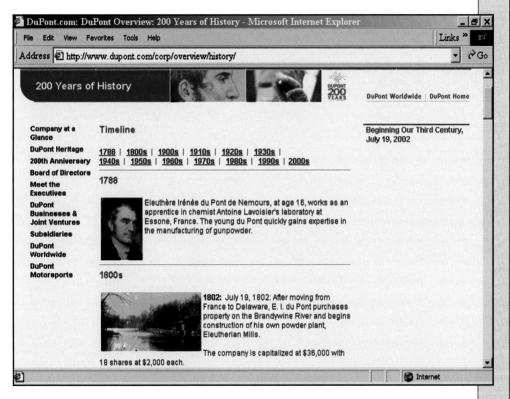

DuPont.com: DuPont Overview: 200 Years of History - Microsoft Internet Explorer

File   Edit   View   Favorites   Tools   Help   Links »

Address http://www.dupont.com/corp/overview/history/   ▼ Go

200 Years of History   DuPont Worldwide | DuPont Home

Company at a Glance   **Timeline**   Beginning Our Third Century, July 19, 2002

DuPont Heritage
200th Anniversary   1788 | 1800s | 1900s | 1910s | 1920s | 1930s |
Board of Directors   1940s | 1950s | 1960s | 1970s | 1980s | 1990s | 2000s
Meet the Executives
    1788
DuPont
Businesses &   Eleuthère Irénée du Pont de Nemours, at age 16, works as an
Joint Ventures   apprentice in chemist Antoine Lavoisier's laboratory at
Subsidiaries   Essone, France. The young du Pont quickly gains expertise in
    the manufacturing of gunpowder.
DuPont
Worldwide
DuPont   **1800s**
Motorsports
    1802: July 19, 1802: After moving from
    France to Delaware, E. I. du Pont purchases
    property on the Brandywine River and begins
    construction of his own powder plant,
    Eleutherian Mills.

    The company is capitalized at $36,000 with
    18 shares at $2,000 each.

Internet

▲ *The DuPont Company was founded by Eleuthère Irénéé du Pont de Nemours, who in 1802 purchased property on the Brandywine River and built a plant, Eleutherian Mills, that made gunpowder. Today, the DuPont Company operates in 70 countries worldwide.*

▲ *The Winterthur Museum, Garden and Library, six miles northwest of Wilmington, was once the country estate of Henry du Pont. The museum also features an extensive research library on American decorative art.*

▶ An Artful Legacy

In addition to manufacturing products that have changed the world, the du Pont family has endowed Delaware with many art treasures and stately homes, including the magnificent museum of American decorative arts known as Winterthur, northwest of Wilmington. Originally the country home of Henry du Pont, the great-grandson of E. I. du Pont, the Winterthur Museum, Garden and Library began as a family collection of American decorative objects and is now home to more than 89,000 pieces. But Henry du Pont purchased more than pieces of art—he also bought entire rooms and had them sent to his estate.

▷ Other Industries

Banking is one of the most important industries in Delaware. Because laws regarding lending money are less rigid in Delaware, many banks have moved their base of operations to the state.

Many large corporations are chartered in Delaware as well. Laws passed in 1899 permit companies to be based here even if they do not actually do business in Delaware. Delaware also has a lower rate of corporate income tax than many states.

Other major employers in Delaware include the pharmaceutical industry as well as the two major universities, the University of Delaware and Delaware State University. Together, the diverse spheres of the Delaware economy have made the state a vital and prosperous place.

▷ Made in Delaware

One of the most famous products made in Delaware today is GORE-TEX, wind-proof and waterproof fabrics for clothing manufactured by W. L. Gore and Associates. These products have allowed mountain climbers to reach the summits of the world's highest mountains with much greater comfort and safety. Many hikers and campers use GORE-TEX products as well. Broiler chickens are another major product of the state. One plant can process more than 200,000 chickens in a single day.[6]

Another product for which Delaware is known might come as a surprise. From the earliest days of piloted space flight, astronauts have worn special suits. Since the 1960s, many of those suits have been manufactured in Delaware by I.L.C. of Dover.[7]

Increasingly, natural resources are playing a large part in the Delaware economy. Nearly one third of the state is forested, and this has spawned a growing wood-products industry. Forest products include sawtimber, veneer, and pulpwood.[8]

Recreation

Recreation is probably the fastest-growing segment of the Delaware economy. Hunting, boating, fishing, and hiking are all popular in Delaware, and businesses such as motels, restaurants, and hunting lodges cater to people who take part in those activities.

Boating, Fishing, Hiking

Recreational boating is popular in Delaware since many people pass through the state via the Intercoastal Waterway, which runs from Maine to Florida. Locals and tourists alike sail on the Delaware and Rehoboth Bays, and recreational boaters also pass through the historic Chesapeake and Delaware Canal.

Deep-sea fishing is available all along the coast. Blue crabs, clams, and oysters are also sought by tourists. Hikers and campers are attracted to Delaware's state forests and parks, which are crossed by miles of trails, and "greenways" are starting to link areas of open space together. The new and expanding White Clay Creek Preserve in New Castle County attracts many visitors as well. One of the largest recreation projects in the state involves the American Discovery Trail. When completed, it will extend from near San Francisco, California, to Cape Henlopen.

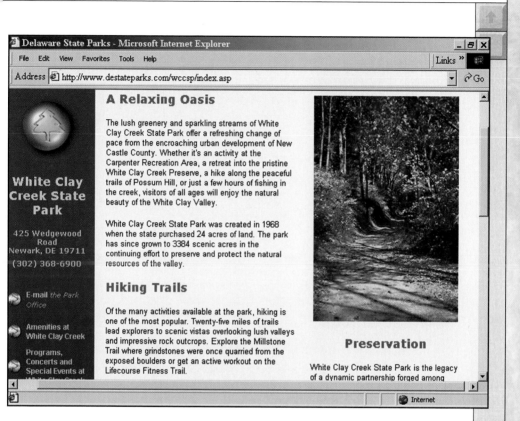

Delaware State Parks - Microsoft Internet Explorer

File   Edit   View   Favorites   Tools   Help   Links »

Address http://www.destateparks.com/wccsp/index.asp   Go

A Relaxing Oasis

White Clay Creek State Park

425 Wedgewood Road
Newark, DE 19711
(302) 368-6900

E-mail the Park Office

Amenities at White Clay Creek

Programs, Concerts and Special Events at

The lush greenery and sparkling streams of White Clay Creek State Park offer a refreshing change of pace from the encroaching urban development of New Castle County. Whether it's an activity at the Carpenter Recreation Area, a retreat into the pristine White Clay Creek Preserve, a hike along the peaceful trails of Possum Hill, or just a few hours of fishing in the creek, visitors of all ages will enjoy the natural beauty of the White Clay Valley.

White Clay Creek State Park was created in 1968 when the state purchased 24 acres of land. The park has since grown to 3384 scenic acres in the continuing effort to preserve and protect the natural resources of the valley.

Hiking Trails

Of the many activities available at the park, hiking is one of the most popular. Twenty-five miles of trails lead explorers to scenic vistas overlooking lush valleys and impressive rock outcrops. Explore the Millstone Trail where grindstones were once quarried from the exposed boulders or get an active workout on the Lifecourse Fitness Trail.

Preservation

White Clay Creek State Park is the legacy of a dynamic partnership forged among

Internet

▲ White Clay Creek State Park, outside Newark, offers a retreat from the industrialized north of Delaware. The park features twenty-five miles of trails and offers fishing in its creeks.

▷ Horse Racing, Baseball, Golf

The entertainment complex at Dover Downs features harness racing and NASCAR races as well as a casino. The complex attracts thousands of visitors each year. There is also horse racing in Harrington, at Ocean Downs, and at Delaware Park.

Delaware is also the home of a Minor League baseball team—the Wilmington Blue Rocks, who play in the Carolina League. And the state is the site of the championship tournament of the LPGA (the Ladies Professional Golf Association), which is played each year near Wilmington.

Government

Some form of government has existed in Delaware since the first settlement was founded in 1638. Early governors served the king or queen of their home country and were given broad powers to rule the people. When the Swedish settled in Delaware, for example, a series of governors ruled in the name of Sweden's Queen Christina.[1] Later, colonial governors would serve the Dutch and English thrones.

▶ The Dutch Influence

The second era of Dutch settlement in Delaware, beginning in 1673, had a lasting influence on the future state. While the Dutch ruled, they established three district

▲ New Castle, Delaware's original capital, hosts an annual festival each May known as "A Day in Old New Castle." Reenactors in eighteenth-century costume give visitors a sense of what life was like in Delaware during the American Revolution. Carriage rides, colonial music and crafts, and historic house tours round out the day.

courts in Delaware. The courts not only strengthened the rule of law in the colony but also set the boundaries for three districts that would become Delaware's three counties—New Castle in the north; the central county, Kent; and Sussex in the south.

Penn and Pennsylvania

In 1682, Delaware's government came under the control of William Penn and the Pennsylvania colony, which Penn had founded. One of the first changes made by Penn was the formation of a new government. He called it Pennsylvania's "Frame of Government." A Provincial Council of 72 members, called Freemen, proposed laws to the General Assembly. Members of the General Assembly were elected by all Freemen to create laws and run the government.[2]

Not everyone was pleased with Penn's government, and Delaware citizens were not happy that they were tied to the Pennsylvania colony. Finally, in 1701, changes were made to give Delaware the right to its own assembly, which first met in 1704. Under this system, Delaware was still part of Pennsylvania, but its citizens had some freedom to govern themselves. This system would stay in place until 1776.

Colonial Government

In 1776, delegates from America's thirteen colonies convened as the Continental Congress, in Philadelphia, to vote on whether the colonies should each form their own constitutions for self-government. Thomas McKean and George Read represented Delaware, but they disagreed about how Delaware should vote. So McKean asked Delaware to send one more delegate to break the tie.

Caesar Rodney was appointed that delegate. He rode by horse through the night to arrive in Philadelphia in time to break the tie between the Delaware delegates. Rodney preferred self-government for each colony, so Delaware voted in favor of the colonial governments drafting their own constitutions.

Two months later, in July 1776, the Continental Congress voted to completely break away from Great Britain. On July 4, the members of Congress ratified the Declaration of Independence. Within weeks, Delaware declared itself an independent state and adopted its first constitution.

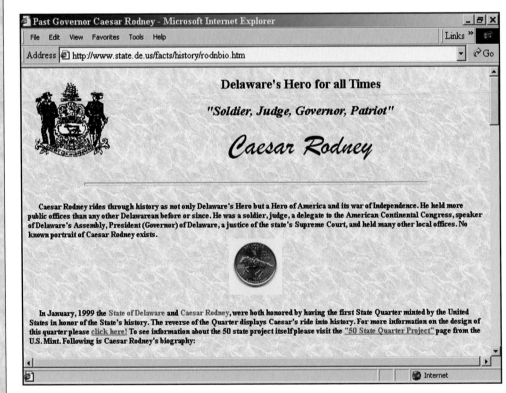

Soldier, patriot, judge, delegate to the Continental Congress, the state's first president (governor), justice of the state supreme court—all describe Caesar Rodney, born in Dover in 1730.

In 1777, Caesar Rodney was named the first president of Delaware. The president of the state would later be called the governor. Rodney served as president until 1781.[3]

In 1786, John Dickinson, who was from Delaware but lived in Pennsylvania, presided over an assembly of delegates called the Annapolis Convention. Delegates representing each state called for a Constitutional Convention in Philadelphia, which was held in 1787. There, the independent states voted to form a new federal constitution. For the first time, all the independent states were united into one country, the United States of America. On December 7, 1787, Delaware's government was the first state government to ratify the United States Constitution, making Delaware the first state in the new nation.

▶ Delaware's Representatives to the Federal Government

Like all U.S. states, Delaware is represented in the Senate by two senators, each serving six-year terms. Because Delaware has a small population, the entire state elects one representative to represent Delaware in the U.S. House of Representatives. Delaware's U.S. representative serves a two-year term.

In presidential elections, Delaware casts three electoral votes out of a total of 538 electoral votes nationwide. The winner of the popular vote across the state wins all three votes. As with representation in the House of Representatives, the number of electoral votes granted to each state is determined by population. During presidential campaigns, therefore, Delawareans don't see as much of the candidates as the citizens of larger states do.

State Government

The state constitution adopted in 1792 abolished the office of president as the state's chief executive. Since then, the head of Delaware's government has been called the governor. A third constitution was adopted in 1831, and a fourth, adopted in 1897, created Delaware's modern system of government.

The legislature is called the General Assembly, and it consists of a senate and a house of representatives. There are twenty-one members of the State Senate and forty-one members of the State House of Representatives. Senators

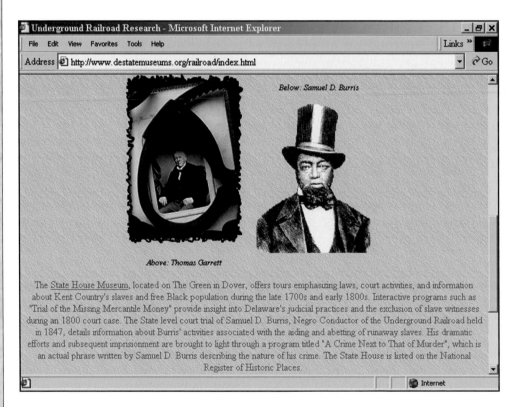

The State House Museum in Dover, listed on the National Register of Historic Places, offers exhibits that trace Delaware's heritage as an important stop on the Underground Railroad.

serve four-year terms, and representatives serve two-year terms.

The executive branch includes the governor and the lieutenant governor, who are separately elected to four-year terms. Candidates for governor must be at least thirty years of age and must have resided in the state for at least twelve years. The governor can be reelected only once.

The judicial branch is headed by the state supreme court, which consists of a chief justice and four associate justices. They are appointed by the governor and approved by the State Senate to serve twelve-year terms. Lower state courts include the Court of Chancery and the superior court.

Dover, the State Capital

Dover, in the central part of the state, is the capital of Delaware. Situated on the St. Jones River, it is also the seat of Kent County. The Delaware General Assembly meets in Legislative Hall, built in 1932. The original state capitol, the Old State House, was built in 1722. It is considered the "symbolic" state capitol and is still used for some ceremonial functions.

Local Government

Delaware is divided into three counties, each of which sets up its government in a different way. New Castle County voters elect a county executive and a county council. Sussex County voters elect a county council, which then chooses a county administrator. Kent County is governed by a levy court, which administers laws set by the state's General Assembly. Most towns and cities also have their own mayors and other elected officials.

▲ Built in 1722, the Old State House in Dover was Delaware's original capitol. Though the General Assembly today meets in Legislative Hall, the Old State House is still used for ceremonial events.

▶ Return Day—A Celebration of Delaware Heritage

Like most Americans, Delawareans take political campaigns seriously, but they like to have fun with elections, too. In Sussex County, an election celebration called Return Day has been held since 1792. Back then, two days after major elections, citizens and politicians would return to town to learn the outcome of the vote. Today, most people learn election results from television, newspapers, and radio, so it is not necessary to come into town to find out. But the tradition continues in Georgetown, Delaware, where voters still turn out for a day of celebration. The highlight of the day is a parade in which the election's winners and losers are pushed through town together in a wheelbarrow![4]

History

Two American Indian groups, the Lenape and the Nanticoke, lived in Delaware before European settlers arrived. The Lenape, whose name means "Original People," lived on the lands of the Delaware River valley. The Nanticoke, whose name comes from the term "Tide Water People," lived in the southwestern part of Delaware and at one time controlled much of the Delmarva Peninsula, so-named because Delaware and parts of Maryland and Virginia all occupy it. The Lenape were later called "Delaware" by European settlers because they lived by the Delaware River. They were not one tribe, but a confederation of tribes who were part of the Algonquian language group. This confederation had three major divisions: the Unami (turtle), the Munsee (wolf) and the Unalachtigo (turkey).

The Delaware Indians were known as fierce warriors, but rather than fight the settlers, they tried to accommodate them. They sold land to the Dutch and later, in 1682, they ceded all remaining land in what became the state of Delaware to William Penn, the English Quaker who founded Pennsylvania. The Delaware resided there until 1720, when an attack by the Iroquois drove them to Ohio. After many more moves, they found a permanent home in Oklahoma. About 10,000 Delaware Indians live there today.[1]

As early as the 1500s, Spanish and Portuguese explorers visited the Delaware coast. The English explorer Henry Hudson, sailing for the Dutch, sailed into Delaware Bay in

▲ *The Nanticoke Indian Pow Wow is an annual event in Millsboro. A celebration of native culture, the Pow Wow attracts more than fifty American Indian tribes.*

1609. British captain Sir Samuel Argall arrived in 1610. Seeking safety during a fierce storm, Argall sailed into a bay protected by a long arm of land known as a cape. Argall named the cape and bay "Delaware" in honor of Thomas West, Lord De La Warr, who was then the governor of the Virginia colony. Soon the river and the land west of it became known as Delaware.

▷ The First Settlement

The first settlement was attempted in 1631. That year, a group of Dutch explorers under Captain David Pietersen de Vries founded the town of Zwaanendael near the present-day town of Lewes. By 1632, however, the settlement had been burned and destroyed by Indians, and all the settlers were killed.

The Dutch were not as interested in settlement as they were in trade, however. Swedish settlers arrived in 1638, under the leadership of Peter Minuit, the Dutch former governor of New Amsterdam. The Swedes succeeded in establishing the first permanent settlement in Delaware, which they named Fort Christina, after the queen of Sweden. The colony took the name "New Sweden."

Peter Stuyvesant, governor of the Dutch colony of New Netherland, sailed to Delaware in 1651 and established Fort Casimir where present-day New Castle now

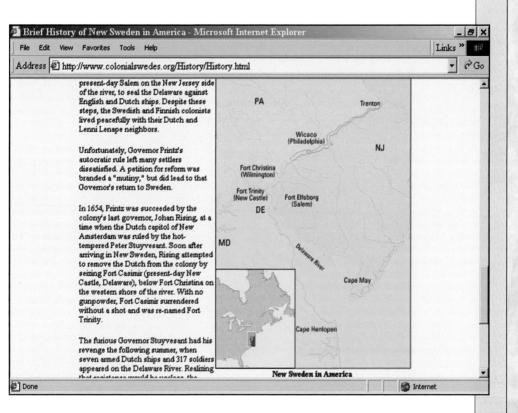

present-day Salem on the New Jersey side of the river, to seal the Delaware against English and Dutch ships. Despite these steps, the Swedish and Finnish colonists lived peacefully with their Dutch and Lenni Lenape neighbors.

Unfortunately, Governor Printz's autocratic rule left many settlers dissatisfied. A petition for reform was branded a "mutiny," but did lead to that Governor's return to Sweden.

In 1654, Printz was succeeded by the colony's last governor, Johan Rising, at a time when the Dutch capitol of New Amsterdam was ruled by the hot-tempered Peter Stuyvesant. Soon after arriving in New Sweden, Rising attempted to remove the Dutch from the colony by seizing Fort Casimir (present-day New Castle, Delaware), below Fort Christina on the western shore of the river. With no gunpowder, Fort Casimir surrendered without a shot and was re-named Fort Trinity.

The furious Governor Stuyvesant had his revenge the following summer, when seven armed Dutch ships and 317 soldiers appeared on the Delaware River. Realizing that resistance would be useless, the

New Sweden in America

▲ In 1638 the Swedes were the first Europeans to establish a permanent settlement in Delaware. The colony thus took the name "New Sweden."

stands. The Swedes captured the fort in 1654, but Stuyvesant recaptured it for the Dutch in 1655 and took over all of New Sweden, making it part of New Netherland. So many new Dutch settlers followed that a second settlement, called New Amstel, was established.

The English Seize Control

In 1664 the English seized the lands on the Delaware River that were held by the Dutch. In 1673 the Dutch regained the colony, but by 1674 the English took control once again. King Charles II granted the land to his brother James Stuart, the Duke of York (later King James II). Eight years later, the Duke granted the land to William Penn's new colony of Pennsylvania. Penn had petitioned the king for control of the lands "west of the Delaware Bay" below his province. Penn had feared that his colony might become landlocked if surrounding colonies became hostile to him.[2] It was at this time that Delaware was officially referred to as "The Three Lower Counties or Territories of Pennsylvania."

The neighboring colony of Maryland, however, disputed the boundaries of Delaware. To help settle this dispute and other land disputes between the ruling families of Pennsylvania and Maryland, two British astronomers, Charles Mason and Jeremiah Dixon, were hired to survey the north-south boundary between Pennsylvania and Maryland and the east-west boundary between Delaware and Maryland. Mason and Dixon surveyed these lands between 1763 and 1768. The boundary between Pennsylvania and Maryland created by their survey is now known as the Mason-Dixon Line. The Mason-Dixon Line was used before the Civil War to mark the boundary between slave states and free states. It continues to be thought of as a boundary between North and South in America.

Delaware remained a part of the Pennsylvania colony until 1776. When the members of the Continental Congress signed the Declaration of Independence, Delaware declared its independence not only from Great Britain, but from Pennsylvania as well.

Delaware's Sons at War

During the American Revolution, Delaware sent nearly 4,000 men to fight against the British. Only one battle, known as the Battle of Cooch's Bridge, was fought on

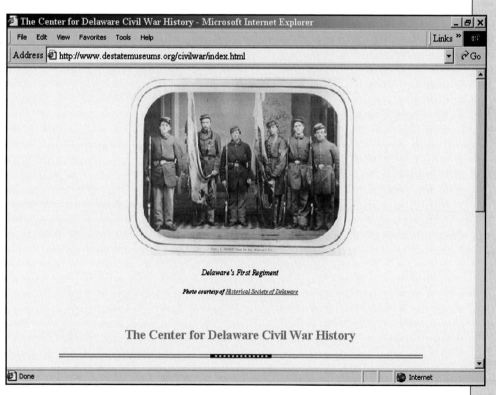

The Center for Delaware Civil War History - Microsoft Internet Explorer

File   Edit   View   Favorites   Tools   Help

Links »

Address http://www.destatemuseums.org/civilwar/index.html   Go

Delaware's First Regiment

Photo courtesy of Historical Society of Delaware

The Center for Delaware Civil War History

Done   Internet

Delaware's situation during the Civil War was unique: Though it was officially a slave state, it sided with the Union, and because of its location, Delaware had ties to both North and South.

Delaware soil. British troops skirmished with Continental Army troops under the command of General George Washington before going on to occupy Wilmington for a month.[3]

During the Civil War, Delaware sided with the Union, even though it officially was a slave state. Because of its location, Delaware had ties to both the North and the South. More than 90 percent of the African Americans living in Delaware at the time were free, though their freedom was limited in that they could not vote. And those African Americans who were slaves were not freed in 1863 by the Emancipation Proclamation. The proclamation freed slaves in the Confederate states but did not apply to slaves in slave states, like Delaware, that had remained in the Union. So slaves in Delaware were not freed until 1865, when the Thirteenth Amendment to the Constitution abolished slavery everywhere in the United States.

The Underground Railroad

Despite the state's divided sympathies, Delaware played a key role in the Underground Railroad, a network of people that helped slaves escape to freedom in the northern states. One Delawarean, Thomas Garrett, helped more than 2,500 slaves on their journey north between 1820 and 1865. He continued his efforts despite threats on his life and despite being ordered to stop by the chief justice of the United States. Today Garrett is honored with a statue in Wilmington. Fifteen sites around the state are now recognized as "stops" on the railroad—places where escaping slaves were hidden on their way to freedom.[4] Woodburn, the official residence of the governor of Delaware, is believed to have been a stop on the Underground Railroad.

▶ The Rise of Manufacturing

By the end of the nineteenth century, the building of the Chesapeake and Delaware Canal and the railroad had improved transportation into and out of Delaware so much that a boom in manufactured goods was created. The DuPont Chemical Company of Wilmington would lead this boom into the twentieth century. Three products, freon for refrigeration in 1931, synthetic rubber in 1933, and nylon in 1938, were DuPont products that changed people's lives around the world.[5] In time, other manufacturing companies would take advantage of efficient transportation on the Delaware River and build factories in the state.

The late twentieth century saw an increasing emphasis on the importance of natural history in Delaware. Major sections of the state's shoreline are now protected as the Delaware Seashore State Park, and areas of open space called greenways crisscross the state. Much has also been done to protect the state's wetlands, with several areas serving as large preserves for the intricate web of life found in Delaware's salt marshes. Even areas where farming is done are monitored so that some natural habitat can be preserved.

The story of Delaware, the First State, is a gateway to America's past and reflects the nation's own story in many rich and varied ways. It is easy to see why Delawareans are so fond of their state. They have got a lot to be proud of: natural beauty, a rich history, a rural heritage, and prosperity. It is no surprise that they refer to their home state as a "small wonder."

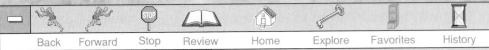
Chapter Notes

Chapter 1. The State of Delaware

1. Borgna Brunner, ed., *Time Almanac 2002* (Boston: Information Please, 2001), p. 145.

2. *Shorebirds: The Delaware Bay Connection* (Washington, D.C.: U.S. Fish and Wildlife Service, 1998).

3. Jennifer Ackerman, *Notes from the Shore* (New York: Viking Press, 1995), p. 4.

4. The DuPont Company, *History of DuPont*, May 7, 2001, <http://www.dupont.com/corp/gbl-company/hist1800.html>.

Chapter 2. Land and Climate

1. Borgna Brunner, ed., *Time Almanac 2002* (Boston: Information Please, 2001), p. 607.

2. The State of Delaware, "Delaware Facts," *Delaware.gov*, n.d., <www.state.de.us/gic/facts/history/delhist.htm> (10/12/01).

3. *Delaware Forests: A Vision for the Future* (Dover: Delaware Dept. of Agriculture, 1998), p. 4.

4. *Delaware Bay Shorebirds* (Dover: Delaware Dept. of Natural Resources, 1998).

5. *Shorebirds—The Delaware Bay Connection* (Washington, D.C.: U.S. Fish and Wildlife Service, 1998).

Chapter 3. Economy

1. The United States Geological Survey, *Historical Information for Wilmington—Economic History*, n.d., <http://mcmcweb.er.usgs.gov/phil/wilmhistory.html> (10/13/01).

2. The State of Delaware, "Delaware Facts," *Delaware.gov*, n.d., <www.state.de.us/gic/facts/history/delhist.htm> (10/13/01).

3. The Boating Information Bureau, "The Chesapeake and Delaware Canal," reprinted from *Sail*, August 2000, <www.boatcom.com/history/082200.htm> (10/13/01).

4. The DuPont Company, *History of DuPont*, n.d., <www.dupont.com/corp/gbl-company/hist1900/hist1900.html> (10/13/01).

5. The DuPont Company, *History of DuPont*, n.d., <www.dupont.com/corp/gbl-company/hist1900/hist1900.html> (10/13/01).

6. *Harris Info Source* (Twinsburg, Ohio: Harris, 2000), p. 56.

7. *Harris Info Source*, p. 47.

8. Delaware Department of Agriculture Forest Service, *Delaware Stewardship News*, Spring/Summer 1997, volume 1, number 2, p. 7.

Chapter 4. Government

1. The State of Delaware, "State of Delaware—A Brief History," *Delaware.gov*, n.d., <www.state.de.us/gic/facts/history/delhist.htm> (10/17/01).

2. "Frame of Government of Pennsylvania, 1696," *The Avalon Project at the Yale Law School*, n.d., <www.yale.edu/lawweb/avalon/states/pa06.htm> (10/17/01).

3. Colonial Hall, "Caesar Rodney, 1730–1783," *Colonial Hall: A Look at America's Founders*, n.d., <www.colonialhall.com/rodney/rodney.asp> (10/17/01).

4. At the Beach Enterprises, "Georgetown—The Home of Return Day," *Welcome to Georgetown*, n.d., <www.georgetownde.com> (10/17/01).

Chapter 5. History

1. The Delaware Tribe of Indians, *Home page*, n.d., <www.delawaretribeofindians.nsn.us/> (10/15/01).

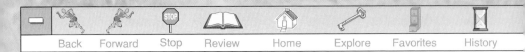
2. The State of Delaware, "Delaware Facts—History," *Delaware.gov*, n.d., <www.state.de.us/gic/facts/history/delhist.htm> (10/15/01).

3. The State of Delaware, "Delaware Facts—History," *Delaware.gov*, n.d., <www.state.de.us/gic/facts/history/delhist.htm> (10/15/01).

4. The State of Delaware, "A Delawarean That Made a Difference," *Delaware.gov*, n.d.,<www.state.de.us/facts/history/garrbio.htm> (10/15/01).

5. The DuPont Company, *DuPont History*, n.d., <www.dupont.com/corp/gbl-company/hist1927/hist1927.html> (10/15/01).

Further Reading

Ackerman, Jennifer. *Notes from the Shore.* New York: Viking Press, 1995.

Dunlap, Julie. *Extraordinary Horseshoe Crabs.* Minneapolis, Minn.: Carolrhoda Books, 1999.

Fradin, Dennis Brindell. *The Delaware Colony.* Danbury, Conn.: Children's Press, 1992.

Hitakonanu'laxk. *The Grandfathers Speak: Native American Folk Tales of the Lenape People.* New York: Interlink Books, 1994.

Hoffecker, Carol E. *Delaware, the First State.* Wilmington, Del.: Middle Atlantic Press, 1989.

Hornberger, Patrick and Joy Waldron. *Lighthouses of Delaware Bay: The Lighthouses and Lightships of Delaware Bay and River.* Trappe, Md.: Eastwind Publishing, 1998.

Melchiore, Susan. *Caesar Rodney: American Patriot.* Broomall, Pa.: Chelsea House Publishing, 2000.

Monroe, John A. *History of Delaware.* Newark: University of Delaware Press, 2001.

Thompson, Priscilla M. and Sally O'Byrne. *Wilmington's Waterfront.* Charleston, S.C.: Arcadia Publishing, 1999.

Welsbacher, Anne. *Delaware.* Minneapolis, Minn.: ABDO Publishing, 1998.